Same Page

A FREELANCE WRITER'S GUIDE

TO BUILDING HEALTHY CLIENT RELATIONSHIPS

Rebecca Livermore

Professional Content Creation

Littleton, Colorado

Same Page

Learn more information at: ProfessionalContentCreation.com

Table of Contents

Introduction

Bar none, client work is the number one way I've made money as a writer. In fact, client work is what enabled me to quit my day job and work from home full-time.

But it hasn't always been easy. I've written content for a wide range of clients, some good, some not-so-good. I'd love to blame all the problems I've had with the "not good" clients on them. And to be sure, some of my writing clients exhibited narcissistic behavior or had other issues that made them complicated, through no fault of my own.

However, it's also true that when it comes right down to it, some of my struggles with writing content for clients was a direct result of not being on the same page with them. They had unspoken expectations, and so did I. When those expectations clashed, problems ensued.

It took me some time to realize that the responsibility to be on the same page with my clients was mostly in my control. I discovered that the secrets to building healthy client relationships start with the very first conversation and build from there.

About this Book

My goal for this book is to help other writers avoid some painful pitfalls I experienced as I built my writing business. The bottom line is that knowing what I know now when I first started would have spared me a lot of pain, frustration, and sleepless nights. It also would have saved me a ton of time and empowered me to make more money as a writer early on.

Simply put, this is the book I wish I had available to me when I first started writing content for clients.

In it I share:

- The importance of interviewing clients before agreeing to work for them, and the types of things to discuss in the interview
- The difference between contracts and proposals and what to include in them
- How to get paid on time
- How to properly train your clients and why your actions carry more weight than your words
- When you should go the extra mile for your writing clients and how to do so without being abused
- How to position yourself to fire clients, so you never end up stuck in bad client relationships
- 5 reasons to let a writing client go
- How to recover from toxic clients
- And so much more

Through this book, you'll learn how to get – and stay on – the same page with your writing clients.

About the Author

I've worked as a freelance writer since 1993 and got my start writing for print magazines. I transitioned to writing for the web in 2006. While I made money writing for magazines and websites, writing content for clients is what enabled me to quit my day job in 2012.

While it's true that I've experienced my fair share of toxic clients, I've also been privileged to work for the best of the best. Among others, I've worked for:

- Amy Porterfield, the queen of all things online marketing. She was my very first client. I still had my day job when I started working for her. During the three years I worked for her, her business exploded, and I subsequently launched my own business. I credit most of what I know and the success that I've had through my time working for her.
- Michael Hyatt, former CEO of Thomas Nelson, NYTimes bestselling author, top blogger, and business mentor taught me so much about how to optimize my blog, not to mention how to balance work and rest.
- Pat Flynn is fantastic when it comes to pretty much everything. His content is excellent. He does an outstanding job genuinely caring for others and going the extra mile for everyone with whom he comes in contact. Through Pat, I learned how to build a content-based business, including affiliate marketing, without being salesy.
- Marcus Sheridan gives hope to all who have something to say but may not consider themselves to be great writers. He was, "just a pool guy" who managed to save

his business through blogging. In addition to helping him start his podcast, I enjoyed editing his content and writing content for his clients.

- S.J. Scott – my relationship with Steve is different than the others in that I have worked with, not "for" him. To date, we've co-written five books. He's a master writer, with a ton of business sense, and an all-around great guy.

Working for each of them was a great privilege, and I have nothing but good things to say about all of them. I am who I am today in large part because of them. Suffice it to say that none of the nightmare stories I share in this book are about any of the above-listed people.

On a personal note, I've been married to my husband, Chuck, for more than 30 years and am the mom to two young adults who affectionately nicknamed me, "Hot Rod Mama." I'll leave it to your imagination to guess why.

Free Gift

I've created a free companion course to go along with this book. In addition to the video content, the course has a discussion area where you can ask questions. You can also upload a project and get my feedback. Since I no longer offer coaching, this is the only way to get individualized feedback from me, at no cost to you. Go here to get your free course: https://www.professionalcontentcreation.com/pw1extras

Chapter 1: Interview Potential Clients

Client work is one of the best ways to make money as a writer. I've worked for some amazing clients. As I mentioned earlier, I've also worked for some toxic clients. Through it all, I've learned the importance of interviewing potential clients. This one step helps you weed out the bad apples BEFORE you ever start working for them.

The Potential Client Needs to Sell YOU

As a freelancer, it's easy to focus on trying to land a client. However, you can expect better results if you turn that around and focus on the client's need to *sell you* on taking them on.

Shift Your Mindset

This doesn't mean that you tell them they have to convince you. Nor does it mean that you shouldn't put your best foot forward in the interview process.

But if you can shift your mindset to conducting the interview rather than being interviewed, you'll avoid coming across as desperate.

Think Back on Past Relationships

Remember how you responded to someone that seemed desperate to be in a relationship with you. Chances are, you felt smothered and just wanted to run away from them. In contrast, if you were interested in someone, and they were decent to you, but a bit aloof, you probably felt intrigued, and more interested.

The same basic dynamic works in business relationships. It's fine to express interest in a client relationship. However, the potential client will value you more if you avoid coming across as needy and willing to do anything to get the job.

It's Better to Eliminate the Wrong Clients

The lack of desperation positions you to negotiate. Also, it's better to eliminate the wrong client from the start, rather than taking on any client out of desperation.

I understand this is difficult at the beginning if you don't have any or enough clients and need to pay the bills. However, the wrong client not only wears you down; they also rob your time to devote to the right clients.

Discuss Needs and Expectations

One thing that I've found helpful in the interview process is to talk with the clients about their needs and expectations. For example:

- What type of tasks do they need to have done?
- What is their work style?
- Do they like a lot of face-to-face or video interaction?
- Do they like frequent phone calls?
- What about email and texts?
- Do they typically take weekends and holidays off?
- What time in the morning do they start work?

Discover if Your Work Styles are Compatible

When you ask these types of questions, you find out whether you have compatible work styles. For instance, I'm an introvert. I'm willing to have a certain amount of phone calls, video chats, or in-person meetings, but I prefer email and text communication.

If I perceive someone wants to have multiple phone calls every week, they're probably not a good fit. In contrast, you may like a lot of face-to-face time with someone and hate to communicate by email or text. The important thing is to determine what works best for you and as much as possible eliminate clients that *strongly* prefer an opposite work style.

Be Honest about Your Weaknesses

Another thing I'd like to encourage you to do is, to be honest about your weaknesses. This is the opposite of what most people do in an interview. This honesty fosters trust. It also helps the client make a better decision about whether you're a good fit for them. Also, if you're honest about your weaknesses, it reduces the chance they'll be upset with you if they later ask you to do something outside your areas of strength.

Break Your Weaknesses into Two Categories

When considering your weaknesses, break them into two categories:

- #1: Tasks you are not good at and have NO desire to do
- #2: Work you don't yet know how to do or are not very good at, but are interested in and willing to learn

For instance, I'm not good at spreadsheets, and I don't like them. Because of that, I'd let a potential client that heavily uses spreadsheets know that I'm not good at Excel.

My Client Paid Me to Learn

However, what if the potential client expresses a need for something I don't know how to do, but am interested in learning? If I feel confident that I can learn the skill, I say something like, "I don't yet have experience with that, but I'm willing to learn."

For example, I once had a client that wanted to start a podcast. I didn't know the first thing about editing audio or getting a podcast on iTunes. However, podcasting was on my list of skills I wanted to learn. Despite my lack of experience in podcasting, my other skills checked the right boxes, and he hired me anyway. He then paid for me to learn podcasting. This worked out great for both of us because I was able to help him launch a successful podcast, and I developed a new skill. In addition to my writing services, I was able to offer podcast production work (including written show notes) to other clients.

Go with Your Gut

Finally, go with your gut. While it's normal to have a little bit of nervousness when starting with a new client, if you have a bad feeling in the pit of your stomach about working with them, it's best to walk away or at the very least, start with a small project rather than agreeing to something big.

Don't be Ruled by Fear

The critical thing is to refuse to allow fear to dictate what you'll agree to and with whom you'll work. If out of necessity you do get stuck doing less than ideal work or work for a less than ideal client, stay tuned, because later in this book I'll share some tips for how to position yourself to let a client go.

Chapter 2: Contracts and Proposals

After the initial interview process, if both you and the potential client agree to move forward, it's time to create a contract.

Proposals Vs. Contracts

As a side note, let me say that you can use some of the ideas in this chapter to create a proposal. Proposals are similar to contracts. They lay out the basics of the work you'll do, along with your terms, but may not yet be set in stone.

After your initial conversation with the potential client, unless you already came to a solid agreement, offer to create a proposal. Proposals are an excellent negotiating tool, and a great way to make sure you're both on the same page before sending a contract. Since proposals aren't legal documents, people may feel less threatened or adversarial when looking over a proposal.

Discuss and Agree on Changes

Once the potential client receives the proposal, discuss and agree upon any changes before creating the actual contract. The good news is, if you've created a proposal, you've already done the hard work of laying out what needs to go in the contract.

What to Include in the Contract

Now let's get into things you'll want to include in your contract.

#1: The Type of Writing You'll Do

The first thing that goes into a proposal or contract are the specifics of what you'll do. Be detailed here and include a list of project tasks that you'll complete.

This detailed list helps keep clients from asking for a bunch of other things. For example, as a writer, instead of saying something like, "Write a weekly blog post," say, "Write a weekly blog post of 500 – 750 words."

You can go into more detail, such as, "Write a weekly blog post of 500 – 750 words. Additional services such as uploading and formatting the posts, adding meta-data, and sourcing images are beyond the scope of this agreement."

Rewrite the Contract Later if Needed

If at some point the client decides they want more work done such as the uploading and formatting, you may need to rewrite the contract to reflect the additional work and compensation.

You don't have to be quite as specific if you're working on a retainer basis since you will likely be on call or expected to put in a certain number of hours for a set amount of pay. But you may still want to be specific when it comes to the types of work you're willing to do, and as we'll get into in the next point, when you'll do it.

#2: When You'll Do the Work

Next, be sure to include when you'll do the work. This is where you'll get into deadlines and the hours you're available.

A critical thing to keep in mind is that deadlines apply to both parties. You need to have deadlines so that your writing clients feel confident that you'll do the work by a specific time. The clients must also have deadlines so that you have a reasonable amount of time to get your part done. For example, for you to deliver a particular product or service by a set time, they must provide you whatever it is you need by a set deadline.

A Personal Experience with One of My Writing Clients

I once created regular content for a very high-demand client. The blog post and other related content had to go live by 7:00 a.m.

The problem was that an entire team worked on the content, and my part was the last part of the workflow. My tasks took between four and eight hours to complete. I often didn't get what I needed until late the night before it was due. As a result, I often ended up working all night to meet the 7:00 a.m. deadline.

I complained about this and pushed to get things in a timelier manner. They did better for a short period but consistently slipped back into old patterns. The problem is that since I didn't include deadlines for them in the contract, I was obligated to get work done on time, but they were not.

An Example of Proper Boundaries with a Writing Client

With my Blogging Your Voice service, I handled this better. I conducted a recorded phone interview with the client to get the information on a month's worth of blog posts. I had the recordings transcribed, and from there wrote the blog posts. Especially since I had to rely on someone else for the transcription and didn't want to pay a rush fee, I stated that I would complete the first post within a week after the interview. If the client pushed back the interview time, that automatically pushed back my deadline. This kept me from having to get it done too quickly.

Set Office Hours

In this part of the contract, you can also include your office hours. It's true; as a freelancer, you may work all kinds of crazy hours. But that doesn't mean you need to be available all hours of the day and night, 365 days per year.

Setting your office hours helps manage expectations. For example, let's say that your client is in the Eastern time zone, and you're in the Pacific time zone. If you state that you begin work at 8:00 a.m. Pacific time, they'll know not to expect to hear from you until 11:00 a.m. Eastern time, at the earliest.

Setting office hours hopefully prevents someone calling you at what is 8:00 a.m. their time, but 5:00 a.m. your time! If you include your hours in your contract, and the client gets upset because you don't answer the phone or respond to an email on the weekend, you can remind them of your office hours as stated in the contract.

#3: How You'll Do the Work

How you'll do the work includes everything from how or where you'll source images, how many revisions you'll make, what type of files you'll provide, the level of research you'll do, the tools you'll use, subcontractors you'll hire, and so on.

If you explain how you'll do something, it may help your client to understand the amount of time the work will take, since it helps them see how much work will go into the project. Also, if you lay out things such as subcontracting, and they try to push you to get something done faster, you can remind them that others are doing specific tasks, and the timeline those people have set.

#4: Cost

Pricing is beyond the scope of this book, but when it comes to cost, here are a few general principles.

Be Specific

First, be specific when it comes to cost. You've already laid out what you will do, and in this section of the contract, you need to specify the cost. Include things such as late fees, the cost for additional revisions, and so on.

When negotiating cost, keep in mind the money you'll have to set aside for taxes. Also, include some margin for problems that come up and things taking longer than anticipated.

Generally, it's best to have a fee for the project or a daily, weekly, or monthly rate instead of an hourly rate. This is challenging if you're doing more general work in addition to writing, such as virtual assistant work where you do whatever is needed.

Expect things to Take Longer than Anticipated

One general rule of thumb when setting fees is to expect things to take longer than anticipated.

Also, include built-in reviews. For instance, if you do ongoing work for a client, limit the term of the contract to six months or at the most, a year. When the term of the contract expires, you may negotiate a raise.

I messed up in this area when I first did client work. Often the work turned out to be more demanding than I anticipated, and I was locked in at too low of a price. Since there was no expiration date to the contract, I could technically work for the same price for years. You can bring up a change in rates at any time. However, having an end date to the contract provides a more natural opportunity to renegotiate compensation.

Terms and Conditions

Before I go further, let me say that I'm not an attorney, and an attorney didn't review this content. Please do your own due diligence or hire an attorney to review your entire contract, including the terms and conditions.

Now here are some examples of what to include in your terms and conditions.

Who Owns the End Product

First, who owns the end product and what type of attribution will there be? For instance, as a writer, I've sometimes written content that had my byline. Other times I ghostwrote content that had someone else's name.

To protect yourself, include a blurb about how you own everything 100% until you've received the final payment.

Use of the Product

In this section, cover how they can use the product. For example, you may say that they can post the content on their blog, but that they can't use it in a book or other product without written permission and/or additional compensation.

Payment Terms and Project Termination

Cover payment terms for things that go beyond the basic costs covered earlier. For instance, include information on late fees or rush fees. Also include an hourly rate if they want you to go beyond what was agreed to earlier, such as extra revisions.

You may also want to include information on what happens if they terminate the project before completion. At the very least, include something about the deposit being non-refundable.

Public Credit and Extra Expenses

You can also include a sentence stating you have the right to list them as a client or to link to the final project such as blog posts you wrote or a book you ghostwrote or edited.

You can also address questions such as who is responsible for other expenses such as travel. If they require you to travel to attend meetings, be clear on who would cover those expenses.

Contract Expiration Date

Also include how long the terms of the contract are valid. What I'm referring to here is the amount of time they have to sign the contract to lock in the terms. This helps protect you from clients that drag their feet and don't sign it or get back to you in a timely manner. If the potential client takes a long time to get back to you, it's possible you took on other work. If a lot of time has passed, perhaps you've raised your rates. Or perhaps if they don't get back to you promptly, that will impact the timeline that you proposed.

You want the right to adapt the due dates, change rates, and so on after a specific date has passed. Therefore, be sure to include an expiration date for the agreement as part of the terms. Naturally, you'll include a place for both parties to date and sign the document.

Chapter 3: Track Your Time and Accomplishments

Whether you work on a retainer or hourly basis or get paid according to the projects you complete, it's important to record the work you do and how much time it takes – even if a client doesn't require you to do so.

The reason for this is threefold.

First, if the client ever does ask you what you've done and how much time it took, you'll have a solid record that you can effortlessly produce. This also enables you to validate any extra charges, if the time you spent exceeded your original agreement.

Second, it helps you get a better grasp of how much time different tasks take. This matters a lot because when you first start, you may underestimate how long work takes, and because of that not charge enough. For instance, let's say that your goal is to make $50 an hour. You anticipate a project will take ten hours, and therefore you charge $500. That's all well and good if you actually get the project done in the projected ten hours. It's not so good if it took you 15 or 20 hours.

Underestimating how much time various tasks take was one of my big mistakes when I first started writing for clients.

Because of it, I often ended up working from early in the morning until late at night – far more hours than when I had a day job.

The bottom line is that it's not the client's fault if you lowballed the time and therefore, the cost. Even if it turns out to be a bad deal for you, you must honor your original agreement.

If you track your time right from the beginning, you'll be better able to estimate how much you can get done in a day, week, or month.

Third, you'll be able to list your accomplishments. Even if you never show the list to someone else, it feels good to see how much you've accomplished.

In terms of how to track your time, you can use time-tracking software. For instance, the bookkeeping software I use, GoDaddy, has a built-in timer. If you don't have a program that tracks your time, a simple spreadsheet works just as well. If you use a spreadsheet, I recommend including the date, how much time you spent, and what you did in that timeframe. Regardless of how you do it, the critical thing is to get into the habit of tracking and recording your time.

Chapter 4: Get Paid on Time

As a writer, you've probably said or at least heard the words, "I've done the work but haven't been paid." I, in fact, heard those words from a fellow writer recently and wanted to pass on to you some of what I shared with her so you can avoid the problem of non-paying clients.

#1: Explain Payment Terms in Advance

First, it's crucial to explain payment terms in advance. Doing so is essential to make sure that you are on the same page as your client. While this doesn't guarantee payment, it increases the odds that there will be no misunderstandings about the expectations.

#2: Start with Smaller Projects

Next, start with smaller projects. This isn't always possible, but if you can do so, it's a lower-risk way to figure out whether or not someone will be quick or slow to pay. This is also an excellent way to test the waters to see if you enjoy working with the person before committing to a larger project or a longer-term working relationship.

#3: Be Paid Up Front for the Work You Do

Next, receive payment up front. This isn't always possible, and some work lends itself better than others to payment in advance. For instance, I've had some clients on retainer and was expected to do certain things every month, for a set amount of pay. When I was doing this type of work, the clients paid me the end of the month for the work I'd do the coming month, so I got paid before I did the actual work.

For one off-projects that I've done, I required clients to pay 50% before I even started the work, with the balance due upon the completion of the project.

While it's better to receive 100% payment upfront, you must put yourself in your client's shoes and remember that they are also taking on some risk. Particularly if you've never done work for them before, they don't know for sure that you'll do the work as promised, so 50% is a good compromise.

Getting half the payment up front doesn't protect you completely, but if the client fails to pay the balance, at least you're not left empty handed.

#4: Only Deliver the Product After Receiving Payment

Next, only deliver the product after you receive the final payment.

If you need to do the work before being paid, withholding the final product until you receive payment is one way to protect yourself. If you opt to go this route, you can notify the client that the project is complete and will be delivered once they submit payment.

This isn't as good of a set up as being paid in advance because you technically run the risk of not receiving payment, despite having done the work. However, if your clients want to receive the work, they will naturally pay you.

#5: Set Up Automated Payment Reminders and Late Fees

Next, it's helpful to set up automated payment reminders and late fees. Most bookkeeping software has this built-in feature.

I like the automated aspect because when the person gets the reminder or receives a late fee, it's nothing personal. In fact, I once had a client who got upset when he got a late payment reminder, and I was able to let him know that it's an automated process. It's still unpleasant, but it helps the client see that I didn't angrily send out a late payment reminder.

If you're going to charge late fees, be sure that those terms are clear, right from the beginning. No one likes that kind of surprise!

#6: Know When to be Flexible

Finally, while automated payment reminders and late fees are helpful, there are times when it pays to be flexible. For example, I once had a client who sometimes struggled to pay me on time.

The thing that made him different from others who sometimes paid me late was that he always communicated with me. If I sent him an invoice, and he was going to struggle to pay me on time, he immediately reached out and explained his situation to me. For instance, once he had just paid a big tax bill and was low on cash. Another time he had just moved and had a lot of expenses related to the move. In addition to reaching out to me immediately and explaining the situation, he also told me when he would pay, and without fail, he did so.

On top of this, he was a delight to work with in general, so occasional late payments didn't bother me.

Chapter 5: Train Your Clients

Do you have clients that drive you nuts? If so, it's possible that it's your fault more than theirs. Let me explain.

While it's true that there are some nightmare clients out there, many of the client problems you have could be a direct result of the foundation you've laid with the client and the patterns that you've established.

For example, if you typically respond to an email from a client within five minutes, that becomes the expectation. Because of that, if for some reason two hours go by and you haven't responded to an email, the client may become frustrated. It isn't that the client is necessarily an unreasonable person. It's more a matter that you've trained them to expect an immediate response.

With that in mind, here are some suggestions for how to train your clients to work with you.

#1: Start by Describing Your Dream Business

First, start off by describing your dream business. For example, you may want to work regular office hours, with weekends off. Or perhaps you're a night owl, and you don't want to start work until noon each day. Or you may want to work only when your children are in school.

You may want face-to-face meetings with your clients, or you may prefer the phone. Or if it was up to you, you may want to work more independently. Or perhaps being part of a team matters to you.

You may want travel to be part of your business, or you may be a homebody and be 100% opposed to traveling.

Perhaps you like working crazy hours for a couple of months and then taking a month off.

While I won't say that you can always get everything you want, and you may at times have to do things that you don't like, it's essential to start off by determining what you really want in your business, because if you don't know, then it's guaranteed that your clients won't have a clue!

#2: Decide Where You're Willing to Compromise

Next, decide where you're willing to compromise. Let's face it; you may want to work only two hours per day and yet have a goal of making six figures. While that could happen, it's also very possible that you'll need to work more than two hours per day to reach your financial objectives.

Or, you may not like to travel, but can handle doing it a couple of times per year if needed.

At the same time that you're determining where you are willing to compromise, you should also decide which things are non-negotiable. For example, perhaps you're willing to travel but unwilling to do so if it conflicts with a special time for one of your family members such as your child's birthday.

#3: Communicate with Clients About Your Preferences

A big mistake that many freelancers make is that they never let their clients know the things that are important to them or if something bothers them.

For instance, you may hate to talk on the phone and have clients who call you regularly. When they call, you answer the phone, but seethe the entire time. And yet you've never told them how you like to communicate.

Can you see how this is a problem? If you've never let them know how you feel about it, it's not their fault they're doing something that frustrates you.

The best time to do this is when you're establishing a working relationship, before you sign on the dotted line. For instance, we've talked about contracts earlier, and I've seen contracts where communication guidelines that include the preferred communication method, limits to the number of phone calls and so on, are all laid out.

You may not want or need to be as formal as to put it in writing, but it's important to express those preferences and boundaries one way or another as early in the relationship as possible.

#4: Enforce Boundaries

Assuming that you've communicated about your preferences and requirements and that the client has agreed to them, you'll need to be sure to enforce them when needed. For example, you may need to remind a client that an agreement is in place that you won't travel when it's a special occasion for one of your family members.

One thing to keep in mind, however, is that you need to know when to be flexible. For instance, perhaps a real emergency arises, and the only right thing to do is to work on a weekend, even though you usually take weekends off.

The bottom line in all of this is that if you're being taken advantage of or in some other way unhappy with your client relationships, it's possible that you've trained your clients to work with you a certain way. It's up to you to retrain them.

Chapter 6: Going the Extra Mile

One way to stand out among the competition is to go the extra mile for clients. Most clients appreciate the extra effort you put into projects, and the times you're willing to go beyond the call of duty. Most will also reward you for your efforts, and not abuse your willingness to work hard.

There are, however, some clients who won't appreciate your efforts or who demand more than is reasonable. The tips below will help you determine how to balance going the extra mile without being used.

#1: Differentiate Between Normal Duties and Favors

One of my clients' podcast was picked up by CBS. In this transition, my client asked me to compile data on all the previous 50+ episodes. This task was a big one, and he offered to pay me for doing it. I declined the extra payment and instead did it just as a favor.

Several months earlier, he asked me to start adding show notes to each episode on YouTube and switching the YouTube video from unlisted to live after the blog post went live each week. This was a relatively small additional task that I did each week.

He offered to pay me extra for doing so, and I accepted his offer. He increased my pay for each podcast episode I completed.

As you can see from this example, in one case, I turned down the extra payment and just did the work as a favor, and in the other case, I accepted the additional payment.

Here's why: In the first case, this was a one-time thing and not something I would have to do consistently. This client was easy to work with, and it seemed reasonable to do this one-time task as a favor. In the second case, I'd have to do the extra work every week. While the additional work was relatively small, it would "feel" big if I did it week after week, without additional compensation.

On top of this, there was another "little extra" thing that he previously added to my workload, without additional compensation. I didn't want to nickel and dime him to death so didn't charge him for that slight increase in duties. But it would have been a bit much to have done both of the extra tasks without slightly increasing my rates. Also, if I agreed multiple times to do more work without additional compensation, that would have become the norm, and it would be harder to ask for more money later. This goes back to the concept of the importance of training your clients.

#2: Consider the Overall Working Relationship

When it comes to determining when to say yes and when to say no to extra work, it helps to consider the big picture of the working relationship.

For instance, with the relationship I just mentioned, you'll note that in both scenarios, the client offered to pay me extra, without me asking. He also had just given me a bonus when he got a sponsor for his podcast. On top of that, shortly after I started working for him, my brother was killed in a tragic accident, and with needing to travel for the funeral and attend to family needs, I couldn't work on his podcast that week. Not only was he understanding, but he also paid me for the work that I didn't do and even sent flowers for the funeral.

These gestures made it clear that he valued the work I did and wasn't trying to take advantage of me, so the least I could do was do some occasional extra work without additional compensation.

#3: Consider Your Personal Boundaries

I've already mentioned determining which things matter the most to you and making those things clear to your clients. The important thing is to figure out your non-negotiables, such as being unwilling to work on Sunday or on a family member's birthday.

When thinking of non-negotiables, it's important to be clear on your core values. Being unwilling to work on Sunday could fit with a core value that's related to faith, and being unwilling to work on a family member's birthday could fit with a core value of family.

Understanding those core values and your non-negotiables help you know when to say no to going the extra mile for a client.

As you can see, there's not a one-size fits all blueprint for going the extra mile for clients without being abused. However, these general principles can help you maintain healthy relationships with your clients so that everyone wins.

Chapter 7: Keep Short Accounts

Another key to healthy client relationships is to keep short accounts. What I mean by this is to deal with problems as they occur. Don't let things fester. Otherwise, you may end up saying or doing something you regret!

Also, if you feel that something may be a bit off, ask! This is uncomfortable but worthwhile. For instance, I once had a client with whom I had a good working relationship. For the most part, things went smoothly, and it was a pleasure to work with him. But on occasion, I sensed that something was a bit off. I reached out to him to see if all was well. One of those times there was a small issue he needed to address, and because I asked, we were able to clear it up. The other time, nothing was wrong. He was simply pre-occupied with other things and because of that had been less communicative.

When I asked for a testimonial from this client, among other things he wrote, "Rebecca is an amazing communicator. Honest, professional, and always a delight to talk to -- both in person and over email."

The bottom line is that communication matters in all relationships, both personal and professional. Kindly speaking the truth and being willing to hear the truth from your clients is a crucial element of healthy client relationships.

Chapter 8: Position Yourself to Fire Clients

One of the best ways to maintain healthy client relationships is to position yourself to fire clients that are less than ideal.

Desperation leads to a willingness to accept abuse.

It's important not to hold onto clients out of desperation, because desperation leads to a willingness to accept abuse or to put up with working relationships that may not be abusive but are less than ideal.

Two Primary Strategies

I've found that there are two primary ways to position myself to fire clients.

Business and Personal Emergency Funds

The first is to build up both a business and a personal emergency fund. You can do this in baby steps. For instance, I recommend a minimum of $1,000 in both a personal and business emergency fund, so a total of $2,000. If you're short on cash due to client loss, you can use your business emergency fund to pay for essential business-related expenses such as web hosting, your email list provider, and so on, and of course, you can use your personal emergency fund to help cover personal expenses.

Grow Your Emergency Funds Over Time

Once you reach $1,000 in each of the two emergency funds, keep adding to them. You could put a percentage such as 5% of all income into your emergency funds until they have enough in them to cover three to six months-worth of both business and personal expenses. If you want to feel really empowered, keep adding to these accounts until you have enough to cover your expenses for a year.

Fear is the root cause of sticking with toxic clients.

This is so empowering because if you're sticking with a toxic client, the root cause is likely fear. When you have money in the bank to cover your expenses, you no longer have to put up with abusive behavior from a client, nor will you be stuck doing mind-numbing work you dread.

Multiple Sources of Income

The second way to position yourself to fire clients is to have numerous clients or sources of income. I must admit that in many ways, it's easier to have one or two big clients rather than half a dozen or more smaller clients. However, the value of smaller clients is that if you lose one, while you may have to tighten your belt a bit, you can likely still pay your bills.

Your Emergency Fund Will Last Longer!

The great thing about this second approach is that if you combine it with the first approach of building an emergency fund, it helps you stretch your emergency fund. As an example, let's say that you have five clients, and each of your clients brings in around 20% of your income.

A One-Month Emergency Fund Can Last for Five Months!

If you lose one of those clients, even a one-month emergency fund will last for approximately five months, since you'll only need to pull out enough to cover the income from that one client. Five months is more than enough time to find a replacement client, and thus you can make such a transition without a crazy amount of stress.

A Bonus Strategy

I told you I was going to give you two ways to position yourself to fire a client, but I want to add a third, and that is to develop a client waiting list. Now you may not have an actual waiting list, but if you have a good reputation, there are likely plenty of people out there who would love to hire you. They may be people that you've done work for in the past that you can contact to see if they need more work done. They may be friends or associates of your current or former clients. Or they may be people who reached out to you when you were too busy to take on more work.

Do Good, Be Visible, Help Others

The key to this final approach is to, first of all, do good work, and deliver it on time, every time. Be visible in your industry and help others as you have the opportunity to do so. If you do quality work and invest in relationships, opportunities will be there when you need them.

A Personal Story

I'm going to tell you a personal story now of a time when these strategies worked for me. I once took on a high-level client. My initial proposal to him was to work on a retainer of $4,000 per month for part-time content management work.

I knew that this would be a high-demand client and that it wouldn't be worth it to work for less. He responded that he was willing to start me at $3,000 per month, and then after 90 days if I did good work, he would increase my pay to the requested $4,000 per month.

Fair Enough

I felt that this was a fair agreement because the lower pay would last a limited period. To make sure that we were on the same page, I asked him the specific things he'd look for to determine if I'd deserve the raise. He told me that it was "all about the numbers."

My focus, therefore, needed to be on improving everything from website traffic to the average time spent on site, to the average number of page views, and so on.

THE RESULTS SURPRISED EVEN ME!

By the end of the 90 days, I had, on average, quadrupled his previous numbers. For instance, rather than the average site visit lasting a minute, after my work that went up to closer to five minutes. How well I did in such a short period surprised even me. He told me many times how much he loved my writing.

I'M NOT CREATIVE ENOUGH?

But when it came time for my raise, he said he wasn't sure I deserved it. He admitted that the numbers were remarkable, but said things like, "I thought you would be more creative."

I WAS AT A CROSSROADS.

I was at a crossroads. On the one hand, I stood to lose the $3,000 per month he was paying me. I knew I had done my part, proven myself, and deserved the $1,000 per month raise. I also knew that he would not respect me if I was willing to work for the lower amount, so after going back and forth with him on this, I quit.

A WEEK LATER HE REHIRED ME AND GAVE ME A RAISE.

A week later, he re-hired me and increased my pay to $4,000 per month.

I told you this story for a reason, and that is that because I had a good reputation, I knew that I could find other clients. I also had other sources of income such as book royalties, so I would not lose all in a financial sense if I let him go. Besides that, I had some money in savings that would help bridge the gap until I replaced the income. Finally, I knew that my work was excellent, and that I deserved the raise.

Be in a Position of Power

Because of those things, I was in a position of power in the relationship. I didn't expect him to rehire me a week after I quit, but I knew whatever happened, I would be okay.

If you're not in a position to fire clients now, work toward that. Gradually build up savings. Take on another client or two. Build your skills and network so that rather than being desperate, you're sought after. With even one or two of those things in place, you'll position yourself to only work with your dream clients.

Chapter 9: 5 Reasons to Let a Client Go

Now that you understand what you need to do to position yourself to fire a client, it's good to set some objective criteria for letting someone go.

#1: Inconsistent Communication

The first reason to let a client go is inconsistent communication. Now, depending on the type of work you do for a client, you may or may not need a lot of communication, so quiet clients aren't always bad.

For example, one of my clients hired me to write three blog posts per week. The posts were all in my name and based on my expertise. Within a small set of guidelines, I could write pretty much whatever I wanted. I knew what I was supposed to do, and I did it, so we didn't need to communicate frequently.

However, there are times when you really need a response. Though you can respect that everyone is busy, a client who won't communicate when required is one you should let go.

Now I'm not talking about an occasional missed email or failure to quickly respond to voicemail because we're all probably guilty of that from time to time. Instead, I'm referring to those who routinely fail to respond to important communication.

The client who fails to communicate as needed can waste a lot of your time, cause unnecessary stress, and isn't worth keeping.

#2: Persistent Panic Mode

It's also worth firing clients that live in persistent panic mode.

Everyone has emergencies or times when a rush job is needed. However, regular panic sessions are unacceptable. This is particularly true since living in crisis mode is often a result of the client's procrastination.

One reason it's essential to let a writing client go if he lives in a constant state of crisis is that he impacts the service you provide to other clients, not to mention causing undue stress.

STORY TIME

For example, I once had a client that didn't do the necessary work to keep his business running smoothly. Every time he realized how bad things were, he hit the panic button. We then all had to spend the whole day fixing things.

One day, in the midst of the panic, I forgot to show up on a webinar that another client was hosting. Thankfully, she was understanding because I had always been so reliable.

That experience was the last straw that let me know that it was time to let this particular client go. I recall this wasn't an easy decision, as income from this client was more than half my total income.

#3: Lack of Integrity

The next issue is when a client lacks integrity.

We all have to determine our threshold when it comes to integrity issues, and only you can determine where you draw the line. For instance, I once had a client who grossly exaggerated things. For example, he spent $85,000 on a premium domain name and in a YouTube video said he spent $100,000 on it. There were other similar exaggerations, and while they bothered me, they weren't to the degree that I felt I should quit over them.

On the other hand, these exaggerations, piled on top of other issues added up to it being a less than ideal fit for me, so I moved on.

In another case, I had a client who refused to take care of his clients. He did website development and charged a premium price. His work was indeed good, but if something on the website broke, he made promises to fix it, and months later, the problem still wasn't fixed. People paid a monthly amount for website maintenance, and since the websites were so complex, they couldn't easily hire someone else to fix them, so they had to put up with broken websites.

To make matters worse, he gave clients my cell phone number, so I got stuck in the middle of the situation. He wouldn't respond to my texts or emails about the problem, and he also wouldn't respond to developers on the team that sought his approval to fix things for the clients.

While this was an obvious lack of customer service, it was also an integrity issue because he seemed to have no intention of keeping his promises to clients, even though he kept taking their money.

So now let's get into some of the reasons it's important to distance yourself from clients that lack integrity.

> *You don't want to be in the middle of stuff that isn't kosher.*

The first reason is that it's not good to be in the middle of something less than kosher. It's beside the point that you're not the one lying (or whatever the situation is).

It's still uncomfortable to know the truth and how it compares to communication to others.

Your client's lack of integrity can reflect poorly on you in a guilt by association sort of way.

> *If they lack integrity with others, you can't trust them to treat you properly.*

Secondly, it stands to reason that a client who lacks integrity with how he deals with his clients will also lack integrity with how he handles things with you.

If others can't trust your client, why should you assume that she will be honest with you?

As uncomfortable as it is to let a client go, I know from experience that firing clients that lack integrity and pursuing clients that treat you and others with respect is worth the discomfort of firing a client that is less than ideal.

#4: Their Business is Going Down

Depending on various factors, you may want to let a client go when you sense their business is going down. On the one hand, there's something to be said about loyalty, and sticking with a client and doing all you can to help salvage their business.

On the other hand, if you depend on the income, and the handwriting is on the wall regarding the future of the business, it may be time to move on sooner rather than later.

It's essential to pay attention to signs that indicate things are getting bad. For instance, I once worked on a retainer basis for a business-focused blog. I was part of the initial site launch, so it was a baby and therefore, unproven business. But the owner seemed to have his act together and paid me and from what I could tell, others on the team well, and initially, on time, every single month.

Several months into this, occasionally, his payment to me was late. I set up automated late payment reminders, which he responded to reasonably fast.

But then late payment became the norm. Every month, my pay was late, and when he received the late payment reminders, he procrastinated.

Tension grew in our relationship. I didn't like doing work and not knowing when I'd get paid, and he didn't like the payment reminders. He always made excuses for why the payment was late, never admitting that he was struggling financially.

One day, when I asked him about paying me, he told me he had to have the brakes replaced on his car, and that he couldn't also afford to pay me – but that he would when he got the money.

Once he was honest with me, I felt more compassionate and gave him some grace. But I also knew that if things were that bad, I needed to plan my exit, and within two months, I resigned.

This was a couple of years back, and when I recently checked, I saw that the website no longer exists.

It's sad to walk through hard times with clients. For some, it may be a temporary hiccup, and it's worth sticking with them. Others may be in such bad shape it's doubtful they'll be able to pull out of it. How long you should stay in a situation like that is a personal decision, but unless you have enough financial cushion that you can afford waking up one morning and no longer having the job, it's best to plan your exit.

#5: Unrealistic Expectations

The next reason you may need to let a client go is if they have unrealistic expectations.

I've had the privilege of working with top-notch, very successful clients. Successful people tend to have high standards and high expectations.

That's not necessarily a bad thing because you learn a lot as a result of working for people who expect the best. But some have not just high expectations – they have unrealistic expectations. If that's what you're experiencing, then it's probably time to let a client go, rather than setting yourself up for failure.

STORY TIME

Earlier I mentioned the client that required me to publish content by 7:00 a.m. even if the rest of the team got things to me so late that I had to work all night to publish the content on time. That was unreasonable, but his unreasonable expectations didn't stop there.

There were some occasions when the team didn't get me what I needed until after the content was supposed to go live. In those cases, I let him know I'd get it done as soon as I could, but since my part of the task took around six hours, it would take a while.

He said he understood, but then within a half an hour, started texting me to see when I would get it done. To be honest with you, while I never said it, I thought, "*It will go live faster if you stop texting me!*"

EXPECTATIONS OF PERFECTION

To make matters worse, one day as they rushed me to get it done, I accidentally uploaded the wrong feature image. The client texted me with a screengrab to point out my mistake. It was fine that he pointed out my mistake, as it was something I needed to fix.

But when I apologized and told him I'd fix it right away, he responded with, "You need to get it right the first time."

Never mind that I had gotten it right, without fail, over 70 times before, and this was my first time to make that mistake. That comment communicated to me that I could never make a mistake, which isn't possible.

In another incident with the same client, he asked for a time estimate for a massive project. He was shocked by how many hours I stated it would take, even though I lowballed the figure. He sent me an irate series of text messages to let me know how unhappy and angry he was, questioning my integrity and competence.

As if all of this were not enough, this same client wanted me to transition from being a part-time independent contractor that worked from home and lived in another state, to working for him full-time, in his office, a few states away. To comply, my husband and I would have to sell our home and move across the country. To make matters worse, I had observed that there was a tremendous amount of turnover in the home office. While some people quit, I also knew that it didn't take much to get fired and judging by my previous experience with him, I knew that I could move and then end up getting fired a month later.

Considering all the above, I let him know I was unwilling to move. He then became angry and even more demanding. Within a couple of months, I resigned.

> *Here's the moral of this story. When it comes to clients with unrealistic expectations, it generally gets worse over time, rather than better. You can have a good heart-to-heart talk with a client, and things may improve. I did that with him on more than one occasion, and while things improved for a short period, there were deep-seated issues that meant we would never have a healthy working relationship.*

If you find yourself working with a client that has unrealistic expectations, I want to encourage you to do what you can to position yourself to fire the client and move on sooner rather than later.

Chapter 10: Don't Burn Bridges

I've ended relationships with clients well, and I've also ended relationships poorly. Here are a few things I've learned through the process about how you can end relationships with clients without burning bridges.

#1: Keep the Lines of Communication Open.

First, be sure to keep the lines of communication open.

Transitions aren't always easy. Sometimes there can be a certain level of tension in the relationship between you and a client when you decide to move on.

The bad news is that when there are tensions, misunderstandings often amplify. Keeping the lines of communication open is the best way to nip misunderstandings in the bud. For example, if your client seems frustrated with you, instead of shutting down or becoming frustrated yourself, reach out to him to see if perhaps you've done something to bother him, and if so, how you can fix it.

These types of conversations aren't always easy, and there is no guarantee that it will go well, but it's essential to do as much as possible on your side to make sure all is well.

#2: Finish Tasks

No one wants to clean up someone else's mess, so more than ever before, when you're about to move on from a client, take the time — even extra time if needed — to get work done.

You may not finish every single project that you started, especially if the project is a long-term one, but do your best to wrap things up, and if you can't finish a project, make sure that it's clear to everyone where you left off and what still needs to happen.

#3: Document Procedures

Regardless of whether you're part of a team or only work directly with your client, if someone else will do the tasks that you've been doing, it's a good idea to document all procedures. You should document processes to such a degree that anyone else can pick them up and follow them.

How you document them is up to you and may depend on your skill set and the resources that you have available. For instance, you may not know how to create screencast videos or may not have the software available to do so, so instead, you may write up step-by-step instructions complete with screenshots. The main thing is to make them complete and easy to follow.

#4: Speak Well of Everyone

Even in tense situations, it's essential to speak well about your client and any other team members. Everyone has shortcomings. Griping and telling others about them seldom solves any problems. In fact, it creates problems.

Also, if you badmouth clients or former clients, people may hesitate to hire you, since what you did to one client, you may very well do to them.

So instead, focus on the positive things you can say both to and about your client and teammates.

Keep Confidences

Depending on how closely you worked with your client, you may be privy to a lot of confidential information. The information can range from "dry" information such as financials to personal family information. Regardless of what it is, if your client hasn't shared the information publicly, you shouldn't either!

Ending client relationships is sometimes necessary. If you follow the advice above, you'll be able to do it without regrets.

Chapter 11: Recover from Toxic Clients

A nightmare client can not only cause a lot of stress, they can also negatively impact your family, your health, and even your other clients.

Because of that, it's imperative to not only rid yourself of clients that drag you down, it's also important to do what's needed to recover well, and to avoid making the same mistake again. Here are some tips for recovering from a nightmare client.

#1: Exit Well

In the last chapter, I talked about not burning bridges, and I focused on leaving in such a way that benefits the client. But exiting well is also for your benefit. If you exit poorly, you'll have regrets and more stress, and it will impact your emotional and physical health.

Because of that, regardless of how bad a situation is with a client, it's important to do everything within your power to end well. This is tough, especially since nightmare clients are likely pushing buttons and driving you to the edge.

However, in the middle of whatever frustration or anger or disappointment you may feel, remember that even though you can apologize, you can never take back your words. Even if you've done a stellar job for someone, if you exit poorly, they'll remember that far longer than they'll remember all the awesome things you did.

Unfortunately, you'll also remember this, and it's the type of thing that can weigh you down, so as difficult as it is, bear in mind that doing your best to exit well will aid in your recovery.

#2. Take Time to Heal

The next thing I want to encourage you to do when ending a working relationship with a toxic client is to take the time to heal. It's hard to take time to heal when you need to pay the bills, but working for difficult people takes a toll, and rushing headlong into other projects and work for different clients before you recover can hurt you and your business in the long run.

The good news is, you don't have to have a lot of downtime before working to get more clients. Just be intentional about resting and recharging in whatever way works for you, whether that's taking a mini vacation, sleeping a little later than normal for a week, or spending some time at a spa.

#3: Attend to Other Clients Who You May Have Neglected

Next, it's important to attend to your other clients that you may have neglected as a result of the demands the toxic client made on you. For instance, did your nightmare client keep you from getting some projects done for other clients? Did you perhaps respond quickly to phone calls and emails from the problematic client and then do less than an excellent job for others?

If so, address the issue with your remaining clients. Apologize if needed and let them know that you've dealt with the problem and will now be more available and attentive.

Just remember that other clients need not know all the ins and outs of the situation. The words you speak could come back to haunt you later, so instead of badmouthing the former client, focus on your shortcomings and how things will be different moving forward.

#4: Evaluate to Avoid Making the Same Mistake Again.

Let's face it– there was a reason that you ended up in a bad situation. I'm not saying that it's entirely your fault that you ended up with a nightmare client. For sure, sometimes they're unavoidable, but it could be at least partially your fault.

As an example, when I first left my job, I took a client that in my gut I knew wasn't right for me. I had bills to pay, and I thought I couldn't afford to be picky, and he seemed nice enough.

But in my heart of hearts, I knew it was a wrong decision, and out of fear, I did it anyway. That situation taught me to pay attention to my gut, and when it's telling me to say no, to listen! Not listening to your gut before agreeing to work for someone is something I mentioned earlier, but I'm bringing it up again because it's such a common cause of ending up working for toxic clients.

A lot of the other things I mentioned earlier, such as the importance of training your clients well also apply here.

The key thing is to take time to reflect on the situation and pinpoint what went wrong so you can do things better in future relationships. I like to work through things in my journal.

Conclusion

Congratulations on completing this book. Now the real fun begins; It's time to lay the foundation for building healthy client relationships.

As a short recap, here are the main points covered in this book:

#1: Interview Potential Clients

While it may seem counterintuitive to interview clients, this step is an essential part of positioning yourself as a professional, worthy of respect. It will also help you weed out clients that are not a good fit, which will help you avoid a lot of pain and frustration.

#2: Create Contracts and Proposals

To avoid misunderstandings with your clients, spell everything out in writing. If a potential client isn't quite ready to sign on the dotted line, create a proposal, laying out the basics of what you'll do, along with pricing.

#3: Get Paid on Time

To avoid getting burned, when possible, get paid up front. If that's not possible, insist on 50% up front, with the balance due upon completion of the project. If you do retainer work, set up recurring payments.

#4: Train Your Clients

You've heard it said that actions speak louder than words, and that's true in client relationships. The actions you take train your clients to expect certain behaviors from you. Be sure your actions line up with your words and your priorities.

#5: Going the Extra Mile

Going the extra mile for your clients sets you apart from the competition. To keep from being abused, keep several factors in mind. For instance, be more flexible with clients that treat you well.

#6: Keep Short Accounts

Even in the best relationships, things sometimes go wrong. If you sense something is amiss, reach out to the client and make things right as needed. If the client does something that frustrates you, instead of letting it fester, tactfully bring it up.

#7: How to Position Yourself to Fire Clients

There are two primary ways to position yourself to fire clients:

- Have multiple clients so you never have too big of a percentage of income from a single client.
- Build up a large business emergency fund.

#8: 5 Reasons to Let a Client Go

Below are the following reasons I recommend letting a client go:

- Inconsistent communication
- Persistent panic mode
- Lack of integrity

- Their business is going down
- They have unrealistic expectations and demands

#9: Don't Burn Bridges

Even if a client has been tough and you've decided to move on, do everything in your power to end well.

#10: Recover from Toxic Clients

Toxic clients take a toll on you. If you've ended up working for a toxic client, take time to heal. Get some rest, recharge, and evaluate what went wrong so you can avoid making the same mistake in the future.

Free Gift

I've created a free companion course to go along with this book. In addition to the video content, the course has a discussion area where you can ask questions. You can also upload a project and get my feedback. Since I no longer offer coaching, this is the only way to get individualized feedback from me, at no cost to you. Go here to get your free course: https://www.professionalcontentcreation.com/pw1extras

---

Thank You

Thank you so much for reading my work. Please consider reviewing this book on Amazon. Reviews help others to find my books and are much appreciated.

Other Books by Rebecca Livermore

To see my entire collection of books, visit:

http://ProfessionalContentCreation.com/books

www.ingramcontent.com/pod-product-compliance
Lightning Source LLC
Chambersburg PA
CBHW051401280526
45784CB00007B/3054